The Final Years
1977 of the 1981
WOODHEAD ROUTE

Michael Rhodes

Published by Platform 5 Publishing Ltd,
52 Broadfield Road, Sheffield, S8 0XJ. England.

www.platform5.com

Printed in England by The Amadeus Press, Cleckheaton, West Yorkshire.

ISBN: 978 1 915984 29 6

CONTENTS

INTRODUCTION 3

CHAPTER 1
Manchester Piccadilly to Guide Bridge 4

CHAPTER 2
Guide Bridge to Hadfield and Glossop 24

CHAPTER 3
Hadfield to Penistone 35

CHAPTER 4
Penistone 46

CHAPTER 5
Penistone to Tinsley and Rotherwood 58

CHAPTER 6
Penistone to Wath Central 74

▦ INTRODUCTION

The trans-Pennine Woodhead Route dates back to the 1840s and rose to prominence after it was electrified with overhead DC electric catenary between 1952 and 1955. Whilst it wasn't the first line in the UK to be electrified in this way, it was the first inter-city main line and as such attracted a lot of publicity. Even though the route was busy and wasn't listed for closure in Dr Beeching's The Reshaping of British Railways report of 1963, its passenger services were withdrawn in 1970. The line then initially remained busy with freight traffic, but as the wagonload network contracted and the number of trans-Pennine coal trains to the power stations in the North West then dwindled, it was decided to close the central Hadfield to Penistone part of the line. This took effect in July 1981, leaving the Manchester to Hadfield and Glossop section in the west and parts of the former through route within the vicinity of Sheffield to the east.

This book is a photographic recollection of the last few years of the line's working life. It is not a definitive history, as several authors have documented the line in great detail, most notably E. M. Johnson in his 1990s trilogy that was published by Foxline. Rather it is the result of more than a dozen visits that were made between 1977 and 1981, in an attempt to capture as much of the line as possible, plus several further visits after its closure to record the remnants of this once-vibrant railway. In that regard, I am indebted to my colleagues Paul Shannon and Kim Fulbrook who have helped me fill in the section between Hadfield and Penistone, as this was effectively only accessible by car and I didn't obtain a car until 1982, which was after the line had closed. Except where they have been credited, all the photographs are my own.

I suspect that I share a feeling that many railway enthusiasts have had – that is of being born too late or having missed the best days of a particular locomotive class or a line. That feeling pervaded many of my visits to locations along the Woodhead Route. It was clear at the time that its days were numbered, as were those of the facilities it served. From my discovery of the derelict Sheffield Victoria station in 1977, to my observations at Wath, Tinsley and Dewsnap Sidings, I witnessed a relentless decline from 1977. This photographic collection seeks to illustrate as much of the line and its connections as possible during that time.

Michael Rhodes
Thurston, mid-2024

Front cover: The driver of 76051 looks at the photographer with a considered expression as he leaves Sheffield's Tinsley Yard with 8T30, a trip freight that is heading to Deepcar. The western end of the sorting sidings here was partially electrified with the overhead direct current system that continued across the Pennines to Manchester.

Back cover: On 15 April 1980, 76049 had a quick turnaround at Wath Yard. It had passed Elsecar Junction on its approach to Wath at 12.11 and is now leaving the yard at 12.50 with 8M17, a loaded coal train to Ashburys on the outskirts of Manchester. The coal had arrived in Wath Yard earlier that morning on the 8T61 trip from Grimethorpe Colliery.

▓ CHAPTER 1

Manchester Piccadilly to Guide Bridge

Once through passenger expresses to Sheffield Victoria were withdrawn in January 1970, the only electrified passenger trains that remained for the last 11 years of the Woodhead Line were the local services from Manchester Piccadilly to Glossop and Hadfield. In addition, diesel multiple units plied the line at its eastern end between Sheffield and Penistone, on their way to Huddersfield, and from Nunnery Junction and past Rotherwood on their way from Sheffield to Worksop. That said, there was still considerable freight activity on the line, which began from the yard in Ashburys; this took over from Dewsnap Sidings in 1981 as the main location for wagonload freight in Greater Manchester. Further out from Piccadilly was the freight only route that ran south from the railway triangle at Fairfield and connected Reddish depot to the electrified main line. This was known as the Fallowfield Loop and after skirting round the south of Manchester's city centre, this also served as a link to the freight terminal at Trafford Park. Reddish depot closed in 1983 when maintenance of the 1500 V DC Class 506 electric multiple units used on the Hadfield and Glossop services was transferred to Longsight depot. The loop line then continued to see intermittent freight trains until it closed completely in 1988 and it has since been converted to an urban walking and cycling route.

Opposite right: A Manchester Piccadilly to Glossop and Hadfield passenger service is seen leaving Platform 2 at the terminus on 8 June 1977. To the left, 45115 can be seen stabled at the station after having arrived on a cross country service.

The Electrified Woodhead Route and its Surrounding Lines

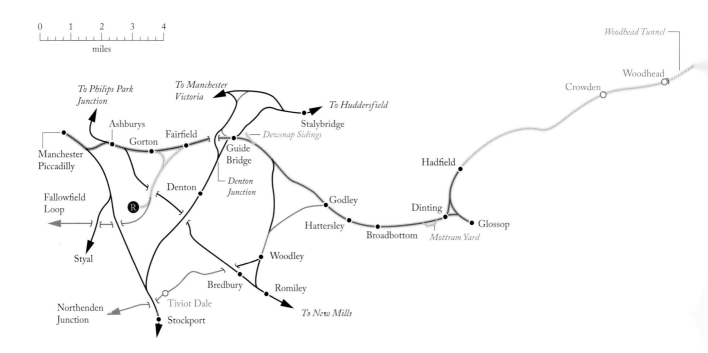

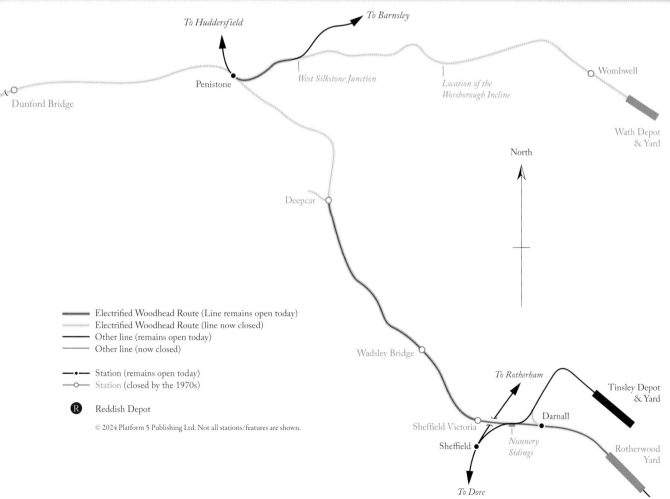

To Huddersfield

To Barnsley

Dunford Bridge

Penistone

West Silkstone Junction

Location of the Worsborough Incline

Wombwell

Wath Depot & Yard

North

Deepcar

Electrified Woodhead Route (Line remains open today)
Electrified Woodhead Route (line now closed)
Other line (remains open today)
Other line (now closed)

Station (remains open today)
Station (closed by the 1970s)

Ⓡ Reddish Depot

Wadsley Bridge

To Rotherham

Tinsley Depot & Yard

Darnall

© 2024 Platform 5 Publishing Ltd. Not all stations/features are shown.

Sheffield Victoria

Nunnery Sidings

Rotherwood Yard

Sheffield

To Dore

Ashburys

Above: On 3 November 1983, I spent the afternoon in the signal box at Ashburys. With the closure of Dewsnap Sidings in 1981, the yard at Ashburys became the main yard for the whole Greater Manchester area. 40174 is seen stabled alongside Ashburys signal box. The original signal box on this site opened in 1889; this had a 62-lever frame and was called Ashburys East Junction. The frame was reduced to a 52-lever frame in the new box of 1906 which is seen here. In 1984, the mechanical frame was replaced by an NX Panel and the box finally closed on 19 September 2011, before being demolished.

Below left: A Hadfield service heads away from Manchester, as seen from the top of the signal box steps with part of Ashburys station being visible in the background.

Right: This second view from the signal box at Ashburys looks in the other direction. It shows 08620 on the left, 40174 in the foreground and 37042 in the sidings in the background. A variety of wagons are visible in the sorting sidings, as seen above 40174. From my recollection the yard had a total of 12 sorting sidings and these were shunted from the west end, with several more sidings that were only accessible from the eastern end.

Left: One reason for my visit to Ashburys on 3 November 1983 was the fact that 76002, 76043, 76048, 76050 and 76053 were all stabled in the old goods yard there, awaiting dismantling for scrap metal recovery. 08524 is seen alongside the retired electric locomotives, being one of two yard pilots at the Ashburys sidings that day.

Above: The mixed freight that 37042 stood at the front of in the top photograph is now seen departing from the yard at Ashburys with 6F45, the afternoon Speedlink working to Warrington Arpley Yard.

Above: Again on 3 November 1983, 45036 passes the sidings at Ashburys in which 40174 can be seen standing. The Peak is heading west with an eclectic-looking westbound engineers' train. It was a bitterly cold day and much of the afternoon was spent taking refuge in the signal box at Ashburys (formerly Ashburys East Junction).

Above: 25239 arrives at Ashburys from the west with the afternoon trip working from Beswick Goods Depot. This image was taken from the end of the station platform at Ashburys.

Reddish

Class	11 August 1975	6 January 1977
24	24005, 24020, 24021, 24022, 24024, 24027 & 24107	24005, 24020, 24021, 24022 & 24024
25	25105	25090, 25115, 25209 & 25277
40	40011, 40042, 40107 & 40117	40020, 40044, 40096 & 40120
76	76004, 76012, 76018, 76021, 76026, 76028, 76030, 76033, 76034, 76036, 76038, 76047, 76048, 76049, 76050, 76052 & 76055	76002, 76004, 76007, 76010, 76015, 76016, 76022, 76027, 76033, 76035, 76036, 76039, 76046, 76047, 76049, 76050, 76051 & 76053

Table 1: The locos present at Reddish depot at 13.00 on 11 August 1975 and at 11.00 on 6 January 1977.

Right: These two images are from the afternoon of 11 August 1975. The main one shows the row of stored Class 24s that occupied these tracks at Reddish for a couple of years, with 24024 at the head of a row of six of the class. The inset shows 76050 with fellow electric 76030 at right angles in the background, as it passes on the entrance tracks to the maintenance shed.

Above: On 6 January 1977, 76002 stands inside Reddish depot's light maintenance building, alongside one of the Class 506 electric multiple units that were used on the passenger services between Manchester, Glossop and Hadfield.

Above, below & right: On a foggy 6 January 1977, the three most common types of locomotives to be found on Reddish depot are captured in the gloom. Firstly we see 24022 after it had recently been withdrawn, whilst 40120 has been cordoned off as it undergoes some electrical testing. Finally 76004 stands with four other Class 76s that had been stabled at the depot over the Christmas and New Year period.

Above: This is another view that was captured on the dull winter's day that was 6 January 1977. After having been at rest for two weeks during the festive period, 76015 and 76033 have just had their pantographs raised in readiness for departure with their first revenue-earning working of the new year. Four of the withdrawn Class 24s stand alongside them.

Denton Junction

Above: Denton Junction is to the south of Guide Bridge; it is the point where the line from Stockport in the south arrives and splits, with an easterly spur to Guide Bridge and a northerly line that goes on to meet the Manchester to Stalybridge line at a more westerly point. One of the passenger trains from Stockport to Stalybridge, which worked every two hours during the daytime, passes Denton Junction on 12 March 1984. The two-car train is made up of Class 108 vehicles 52045 and 51930.

Below: Coke from Monkton Coke Works on Tyneside passes Denton Junction on its way to Northwich where it will be used at the ICI works there. 40004 arrived in the North West using the Standedge Route, before leaving the line to Manchester at Ashton Moss Junction and avoiding Guide Bridge altogether. At Stockport the train will diverge from the West Coast Main Line (WCML) at Edgeley Junction and make its way to Northwich via Altrincham.

Above: With the signal box seen in the previous photograph just out of sight on the right, heading south past Denton Junction on 12 March 1984 is 47266 with a stone train from Peak Forest to Bletchley. Having wound its way north via Romiley, it has just passed through Guide Bridge and will now head back south towards Stockport, where it will join the WCML and use this to reach Bletchley. On the right is the trackbed for the second of the two lines that bypassed Guide Bridge, this being the direct route to Stalybridge via Hooley Hill that closed in 1968.

Above: Freight traffic in Greater Manchester was always a convoluted affair and no more so than in the case of the daily Asburys to Warrington Arpley Yard trip freight. Again on 12 March 1984, 37149 passes in front of Denton Junction's signal box (just out of sight on the right) with the daily working. This had begun by heading west from Ashburys, which is in the opposite direction to where Denton Junction lies. It then veered north, before turning east at Baguley Fold Junction from where it travelled to Ashton Moss Junction, at which point it turned south and passed over the Woodhead Route just west of Guide Bridge. From here the train will travel to Stockport via Edgeley Junction and then reach Warrington using the direct line to Latchford Junction which closed on 7 July 1985.

Above: On 12 March 1984, the 1888-constructed Denton Junction signal box still had gas lighting to illuminate its 54-lever frame. Later that year the frame was reduced to 18 levers, when lever numbers 1 to 36 were removed. This photograph has an interesting history in that after my 1984 visit, I forwarded an 8 x 10 inch copy of the image to the signalman who had allowed me into the box. Fast forward to 2012 and I was visiting Great Rocks Junction signal box when the Local Operations Manager (LOM) unexpectedly turned up to make a visit. The signalman on duty was a bit nervous about my presence and began to explain to the LOM who I was, but he was interrupted by the LOM who announced "I know exactly who this is, its Dr Michael Rhodes!" It transpired that the LOM was Anthony Macintyre, who was the signalman when I visited Denton Junction 28 years earlier in 1984. Over a welcome cup of tea it became clear that his main concern was not my presence, but that he had lost my black and white print in a house move and wondered if I could send him another. An electronic version was sent the very next day!

Guide Bridge Stabling Point

Above: As 8 June 1977 was a weekday, there were only eight locomotives stabled at Guide Bridge. The three Class 40s found on the depot were 40098 and 40174, which are seen alongside 47209 in the first photograph. Looking from the opposite direction, we see 40172 with the sun on its nose, standing behind 40174. The other four locomotives present were 47555, 76033, 76035 and 76049.

These three images of 76035 and 76033 record an unusual short trip working for the pair. On 8 June 1977 they were to be found resting on Guide Bridge stabling point in the afternoon sun and then they were recorded leaving as light engines to head east towards Dewsnap Sidings. Just 20 minutes later they passed with an air-braked freight made up of BBA steel wagons carrying steel bar that was later seen at Ashburys Goods Depot. That was electric super power for a five-mile trip freight!

Above: As the afternoon of 8 June 1977 wore on, locomotive after locomotive arrived at the stabling point after having deposited their freight trains at Dewsnap Sidings to the east of Guide Bridge. Here we see the non-multiple working fitted 76046 arriving at Guide Bridge.

Above: On the same afternoon, 76007 and 76012 pass Guide Bridge station as they make their way towards Mottram Yard where they will pick up a freight train that is destined for the Yorkshire side of the Pennines.

Above: This close-up view of 76040 stabled at Guide Bridge with its two pantographs lowered on 11 June 1977 includes a variety of details. Notice the works plate beneath its number, which reminds us that it was built locally in locomotive works in Gorton and the large number of rivets that can be seen on its bodyside.

Above: As 11 June 1977 was a Saturday, more locomotives were stabled in the sidings at Guide Bridge than what I had found three days earlier. On the left is 76029, with 76016, 76014 & 76049 lined up behind, while the front of 76041 can be seen on the right.

Class	11 June 1977	1 January 1981
08	None	08298, 08477, 08599, 08611 & 08820
25	25119, 25195 & 25297	25143 & 25193
40	40003, 40020, 40042 & 40107	40028, 40073, 40076, 40087, 40107, 40120 & 40122
47	None	47192, 47228, 47232, 47306, 47344 & 47446
76	76011, 76014, 76016, 76029, 76040, 76041, 76049 & 76052	76006, 76007, 76009, 76014, 76015, 76026, 76031, 76037 & 76040

Table 2: The locomotives that were present at Guide Bridge stabling point at 12.45 on 11 June 1977 and at 14.00 on 1 January 1981.

Right: This alternative view of Guide Bridge stabling point on 11 June 1977 illustrates the variety of traction that could be seen there. From left to right are 76052, 76011, 25119, 40003 and 40107.

Above: Moving forward a few years to New Years' Day in 1981 and there were plenty of locomotives present, as Table 2 illustrates. Of the 29 different examples that I noted, we see 76014, 76007 and 47232 sandwiched between a variety of their colleagues in this view.

Freight & Passenger Traffic

Above: 25249 approaches Guide Bridge station from the east with a short unfitted freight which looks to have come down the line from Stalybridge. Note the five or six "spotters", young and old, on this particular Wednesday afternoon.

Below: On 8 June 1977, 40199 is seen heading away from Guide Bridge station and towards the stabling point with a lengthy mixed freight that is travelling from Warrington Arpley Yard to Dewsnap Sidings.

Above: Two views of 25060 as it passes Guide Bridge on 8 June 1977 with a mixed freight that is bound for Dewsnap Sidings. At the front of the consist is a string of empty BEV steel carriers which will eventually return over the Pennines to the steel mills of Sheffield.

Below: Before there were any trains that connected the lines that served Manchester's Piccadilly and Victoria stations, the two-hourly Stockport to Stalybridge services provided a means by which passengers could travel by train across the city. On 8 June 1977, the two-car unit providing this service comprised Class 108 vehicles 56253 and 50981, and this is seen leaving Guide Bridge.

Above: On 12 March 1984, a Class 506 EMU enters Guide Bridge station with a Manchester-bound train. Note the public toilets on the platform and the resident station staff, facilities that are now long gone from most of the UK's stations.

Dewsnap Sidings

Above: The sidings at Dewsnap were to the east of Guide Bridge station. They were difficult to access and even more difficult to photograph. The best views were from the window of a passing train, as was the case here on 4 January 1980. Bumping along at around 50 mph on an electric unit, most of my attempts at capturing the vast array of sidings here were far from perfect. 08640 is seen at the yard neck and whilst camera shake is evident, the image does give a good impression of the yard. There were 53 single-ended sorting sidings here, which in their heyday dispatched freights all over the country, the destinations of which included the major yards at Tinsley, Wath, Frodingham, Whitemoor, not to mention over a dozen further yards in the Manchester area.

Above: Just a year later, in January 1981, and Dewsnap Sidings had closed and was full of derelict and withdrawn wagons. Today the site is a large industrial estate which sits either side of the line that continues east towards Hadfield and Glossop. Unfortunately, the lighting masts were not the type that could be climbed to gain a good overall view of the sidings, as the tall post on the right of the image showing the derelict MCO coal wagons illustrates.

CHAPTER 2

Guide Bridge to Hadfield and Glossop

Godley Junction

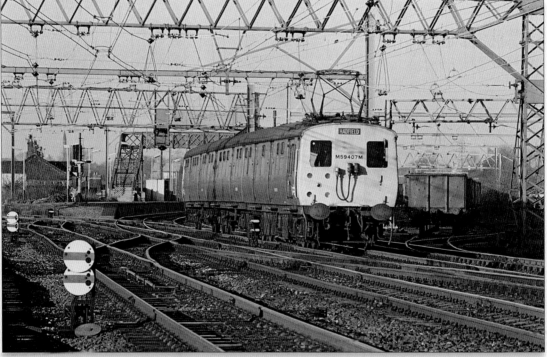

Above: For each of the three-car Class 506 sets, their individual vehicle numbers all ended with the same two digits in the xxx01 to xxx08 series, giving rise to the eight units being known as sets 01 to 08. Here we see set numbers 06 & 07 from two different points as they pass Godley Junction with services between Manchester and Hadfield on 4 January 1980. The line arriving from left is the freight route from Stockport Tiviot Dale via Woodley which closed is 1981. The signal box here was originally erected in 1876 and then replaced by a newer structure in 1916. The later box was equipped with a 44-lever frame and closed in December 1984.

Above: Again on 4 January 1980, 47350 comes off the Tivot Dale line with a train of empty merry-go-round (MGR) wagons that is travelling from Fiddlers Ferry Power Station to Wath Yard. The pantographs of 76011 and 76029 can be seen behind the tenth wagon of the train, as they await a mixed freight from Warrington to arrive, which they will take forward to Tinsley. 47350 will be replaced by electric traction at Mottram Yard, a couple of miles further east.

Below: This and the next few shots at Godley Junction were also taken on 4 January 1980. 76051 arrives ahead of it taking an unfitted mineral service across the Pennines to Wath Yard. It is backing down past Godley Junction signal box towards Brookfold where it will be stabled until its train arrives.

Above: Brookfold stabling point was a couple of hundred yards from Godley Junction, on the start of the freight line that diverged there and travelled west to Woodley and on to Northenden Junction. The line to Woodley closed in 1981 along with the Woodhead Route. When the Woodhead Route was electrified in 1954, Brookfold became an important location because traffic on the Cheshire Lines Committee (CLC) route to and from Woodley Junction would change engines there, with steam being exchanged for electric traction and vice versa. Here we see 76051, with 76011 and 76029 stabled in the background. Brookfold signal box opened in 1915 to replace an older 1883 vintage structure, and it controlled the exchange sidings and passing loop. It was the first signal box on the line to Stockport Tiviot Dale and would close in July 1983.

Above: A Manchester-bound train is seen while looking across the field from Brookfold. It is travelling west (to the left), away from Godley Junction and towards Newton for Hyde.

Above: Again on 4 January 1980, 40022 has arrived at Brookfold with an empty rake of unfitted mineral wagons which it has just been uncoupled from. It stands beside its electric replacement, 76051. Once the electric locomotive has been attached to the wagons it will take these across the Pennines and on to Wath.

Above: The remains of the 20 sorting sidings of Mottram Yard lie to the left of this image which was taken on 16 June 1981. Opened in 1935, the yard sorted predominantly eastbound traffic and eased the pressure on Dewsnap Sidings near Guide Bridge. The yard closed in 1971 and the reception sidings, out of view behind the photographer, closed to traffic in 1980. A Hadfield-bound service that is made up of vehicles M59408M, M59508M and M59608M hurries past the derelict yard. *Paul Shannon*

Dinting

Opposite & above: These two photographs show the train that 76051 took forward from Godley Junction (see the photograph on page 27). Firstly we see it coming off Dinting Viaduct and entering the triangular Dinting station and the second image sees the train heading uphill towards Hadfield. 76051 is hauling a long rake of empty unfitted MCO 16-ton mineral wagons from Glazebrook to Wath Yard.

Right: This classic vantage point shows an eastbound train coming off Dinting Viaduct, as seen from the end of the platform at Dinting station on 4 January 1980. 76011 and 76029, which were attached to this train from Warrington Arpley Yard at Godley Junction, are taking the mixed freight to Tinsley.

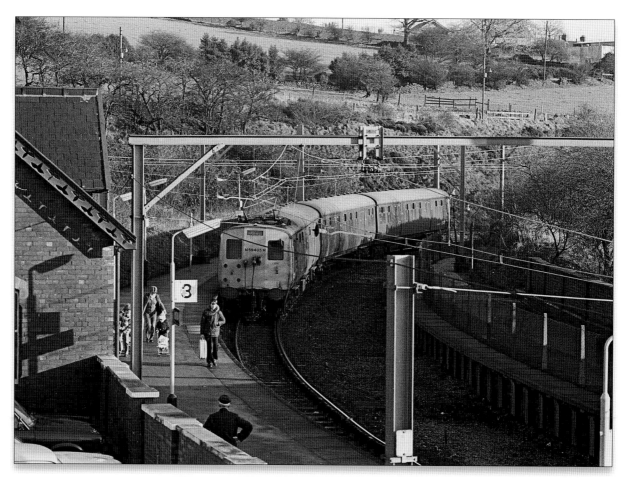

Above: Also on 4 January 1980, we have now rotated to look away from Dinting in the opposite direction. A Class 506 EMU heads along the single track branch to Glossop with a daytime service from Manchester Piccadilly, while a member of the station staff looks on.

Above: From the vantage point of Dinting station's footbridge on 4 January 1980, 76030 & 76014 arrive from the Hadfield direction with a heavily-laden coal train that is travelling from Wath to Fiddlers Ferry Power Station.

Above & below: The low angle from which these two pictures of the same train were taken has produced these compelling views. On 4 January 1980, the consecutively-numbered 76027 and 76028 pass through Dinting with 8M17, a loaded coal working from Wath Yard that is heading to Ashburys.

Above: On 8 July 1983, the 18.58 Hadfield–Manchester Piccadilly began by travelling from Hadfield to Glossop, before reversing there and continuing to Manchester. The train comprised vehicles M59404M, M59504M & M59604M, which are seen rounding the eastern curve at Dinting that avoids the station. *Paul Shannon*

Above: On 25 March 1981, 76007 and 76012 head west towards Hadfield station with 8M17, a coke train from Monckton to Northwich. The consist includes six MCV vacuum-fitted 16-ton mineral wagons, ten MCO unfitted minerals and three HTO unfitted 21-ton coal hopper wagons, finished off with a CAO unfitted guard's van. The signal box was one of the more modern examples along the Woodhead Route. Built to a London Midland design in 1964, it contained 30 levers and survived until December 1984. The view looking east from Hadfield station is now very different, with it being well over four decades since the final trains ran that way. *Paul Shannon*

Above: Class 506 set number 07 arrives at Glossop on 4 January 1980. The layout of Glossop station had been heavily rationalised by 1980, with the wasteland that now lies both to the left and the right of the remaining single track giving an indication of where a variety of additional running lines used to be.

▨ CHAPTER 3

Hadfield to Penistone

The section of line from Hadfield to Penistone was the most inaccessible part of the Woodhead route and one that I never photographed for the simple reason that I only got my first car in 1982, which was just after this central part of the line had closed. I am therefore indebted to my fellow photographers Paul Shannon and Kim Fulbrook for their images which cover this section of the line. Our exploration will continue eastwards from Hadfield as we progressively examine the route towards South Yorkshire.

Below: 76009 & 76023 approach Hadfield with a loaded Wath Yard to Fiddlers Ferry Power Station coal train that is made up of 30 HAA hoppers. In the distance is Valehouse signal box, which was only a mile from Hadfield. This opened in 1896 with 21 levers and closed on 20 July 1981 when the line was shut. The two Class 76s passed this point again less than 30 minutes later, suggesting they came off this train at Mottram Yard where the former reception sidings were used for engine changes on MGR traffic. *Paul Shannon*

Above: During the final years of the Woodhead Route there were two westbound freightliner workings each day. 4M55 travelled from Newcastle to Trafford Park, whilst a second service ran between Stourton near Leeds and Garston near Liverpool. On 16 June 1981, 76021 and 76026 pass Torside signal box with the westbound freightliner service for Garston. The signal box was opened in 1909 and contained 34 levers. It was closed with the line through this point in July 1981. *Paul Shannon*

Below left: On 19 June 1981, 76011 and 76009 approach Torside Crossing with a lengthy load of Yorkshire coal which they are moving from Wath Yard to Dewsnap Sidings, from where it will be distributed around the Greater Manchester area. *Paul Shannon*

Above: Again on 19 June 1981 and a solitary 76051 heads east past Torside signal box. The train is 8E08, the 10.11 Wallerscote–Rockware Sidings in Doncaster and is made up of empty soda ash covhop wagons. *Paul Shannon*

Left: On 19 June 1981, less than a month before the line here closed, 76040 passes Crowden with 8E11, a mixed freight from Dewsnap Sidings to Tinsley. The train is almost entirely made up of 16-ton mineral wagons which are loaded with scrap metal that is bound for Aldwarke near Rotherham. *Paul Shannon*

Below left: 76035 passes Woodhead signal box, which was located at the western end of the Woodhead Tunnel. The box opened in 1953 at the time the new Woodhead Tunnel was completed and the line was electrified. It had a 45-lever frame and closed with the line on 20 July 1981. The train is 8E46, the 07.30 Warrington Arpley Yard–Tinsley and amongst its varied load is some withdrawn parcels stock, at the rear of the formation. *Paul Shannon*

Above: On 8 January 1981, 76025 and 76030 emerge from the Woodhead Tunnel with a westbound coal train. This photograph was taken from the same location from which the previous view of 8E46 was captured, but looks in the other direction. Lurking on the station platform is a young Paul Shannon! *Kim Fulbrook*

Above: Another rake of coal empties returns to Wath Yard behind 76006. This view was captured on 8 January 1981 and shows the remains of the once extensive Dunford Bridge Marshalling Yard on the left. The yard here was a hump yard with four arrival tracks and 16 sorting sidings. In 1928 there were an astonishing 104 different arrivals to the yard over a single 24-hour period. During the 1960s, traffic was concentrated either side of the yard, travelling instead to Dewsnap Sidings, Mottram and Penistone and by the time the Woodhead Route closed in 1981 the land occupied by the former yard was derelict. *Kim Fullbrook*

Above right: The marshalling yard at Dunford Bridge was used to classify eastbound traffic in much the same way as Mottram Yard handled westbound traffic. It closed in 1956, as did the two main signal boxes which controlled the sidings. On 19 June 1981, 76032 and 76034 pass Dunford West signal box with an empty MGR train from Fiddlers Ferry Power Station to Wath Yard. The signal box beside the leading loco opened in 1954 and had 50 levers. Like all the railway infrastructure along this stretch of the line, it closed on 20 July 1981. *Kim Fullbrook*

Right: Looking away from the signal box at Dunford West and into the gloom of the Woodhead Tunnel, 76051 is seen exiting the tunnel with coal empties for Wath Yard on 8 January 1981. *Kim Fullbrook*

Above: This view of Dunford West signal box shows its 50-lever frame very well. On 8 January 1981, 76039 and 76037 head west past the box with 30 MCO 16-ton mineral hoppers that are laden with Yorkshire coal. *Paul Shannon*

Above right: Dunford Bridge lies at the eastern end of the Woodhead Tunnel. On 18 June 1981, an unusual trio were photographed passing the signal box at Dunford East. 76007 and 76012 are towing 45034 which had failed and was being taken back to its parent depot at Tinsley in Sheffield. *Paul Shannon*

Right: This fascinating view at Dunford East clearly shows that its signal box was derelict. It opened in 1900 with a 24-lever frame and is listed as closing in July 1981, but this view from 18 June 1981 suggests that it was switched out and vandals had got to it during the line's final months. Even though many windows have been broken, the block instruments and levers can be made out inside. 76010 and 76016 are passing with 8M29, the 03.25 from Mansfield Coal Concentration Sidings to Garston, from where the coal will be exported to Northern Ireland. *Paul Shannon*

Above: 76034 and 76032 pass through Dunford Bridge station with another heavy load of coal. Their train is 6M51, the 10.40 Wath–Fiddlers Ferry Power Station. The wasteland behind the train is where the marshalling sidings used to be. *Paul Shannon*

Below: One of nearly a dozen ferry trains that travelled to Harwich Parkeston Quay was 6E85, the 18.01 Trafford Park–Harwich. 76011 and 76009 haul this on 17 June 1981, with the consist including a variety of air-braked Speedlink wagons and some ferry vans that are being returned to the port. *Paul Shannon*

Above: The classic Woodhead traffic during the final years of the line was a 30-wagon MGR train that was hauled by a pair of Class 76s. Here we see 76031 and 76037 passing Thurlstone with 6M22, the 15.10 Wath Yard–Fiddlers Ferry Power Station on 19 June 1981. *Paul Shannon*

▨ CHAPTER 4

Penistone

Penistone was very much the central point on the Woodhead system, with lines radiating west to Manchester, north to Huddersfield, east to Wath and Barnsley, and south to Sheffield. It was also accessible by rail which allowed several visits during the last couple of years of the Woodhead Route.

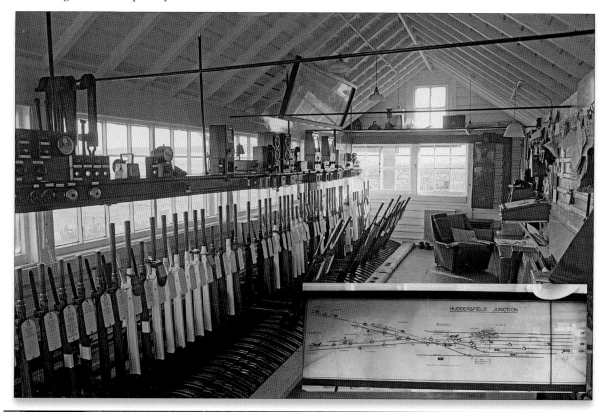

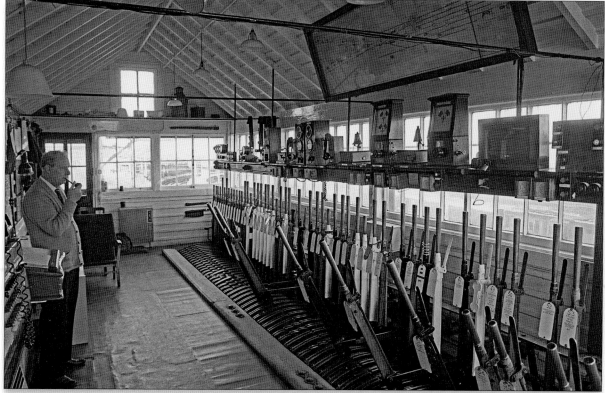

Opposite page: These two views of Huddersfield Junction signal box were taken on 29 October 1980, with the track diagram inserted on the first picture. Sadly the signalman's name was not recorded for posterity, as he welcomed me into the box and made me a mug of tea while he smoked his pipe and we chatted. The box opened in 1887, replacing a short-lived smaller structure that was built in 1884. Initially it had 64 levers but by 1933 this had been expanded to 68. The box survived the closure of the line from Manchester but went on to close in April 1998.

Below: The elevated vantage point for these two views was Huddersfield Junction signal box on 29 October 1980. They show 76007 with what was reported to the signalman as 8M29, an unfitted freight from Deepcar to Dewsnap Sidings. Looking at the load of coking coal, it seems more likely that the train would have originated from Rotherwood Sidings, as they were adjacent to Orgreave Coke Works. Note how many running lines there were at this once-important four-way junction.

Above: Here we can see how high Huddersfield Junction signal box stands, as 76054 approaches from the Sheffield direction with 8M22, the lunchtime mixed freight from Tinsley to Dewsnap Sidings, again on 29 October 1980.

Right: Class 101 vehicles 51496 and 51431 cross Penistone Viaduct with an afternoon Huddersfield to Sheffield service on 29 October 1980. After it has left Penistone behind, the train will reverse at Nunnery Junction, before descending into Sheffield Midland station.

Above: On 29 October 1980, 76021 and 76008 wind across Huddersfield Junction, where the lines from Sheffield and Wath converge, with 8M17, a Wath to Ashburys freight. The silhouette of the signalman can be seen within the box and the sun has also illuminated the face of the train's driver.

Above: Taken from the embankment adjacent to Barnsley Junction signal box, this view shows 76033 and 76038 as they wind out of Barnsley Junction Yard with 6M55, a loaded coal working for Fiddlers Ferry Power Station. The coal is from Dodworth Colliery and had been tripped up to Penistone in two short trains of 15 HAA hoppers that were hauled by a Class 37.

Above: Looking west from Huddersfield Junction signal box and towards Penistone station sees 76037 and 76031 approaching with 8E46, a mixed freight from Warrington Arpley Yard to Doncaster Belmont Yard on 29 October 1980. The train is passing between the two disused platforms that Manchester to Sheffield trains called at until 1970, while the curved platforms that the Huddersfield trains use can just be made out behind the locomotives' pantographs.

The next series of images were taken at Penistone Goods as the sun was setting on 29 October 1980. This location was about 800 yards west of the station; the signal box was known as Penistone Goods and opened in 1899 with a 26-lever frame and closed on 20 July 1981.

Below left: 76028 and 76026 head towards Penistone station with 6M33, an empty MGR working that is returning coal empties from Fiddlers Ferry Power Station to Wath Yard.

Above & below: These two views of 76022 were taken at 15.32 and were the last shots of the day. The locomotive is running with headcode 6Z46, the Z indicating that it is hauling a special working. The empty car flats were being taken to Immingham Docks where they will be loaded with imported cars. The colour image shows the train a moment later, as it passes the old goods shed and heads towards Penistone station.

Above: 76051 passes with 8E11, a mixed freight from Dewsnap Sidings to Tinsley Yard. Whilst technically this is a mixed freight working, the consist is in fact made up entirely of empty 16-ton mineral wagons.

Below: On 17 June 1981 the box at Penistone Goods had just over a month of life left. 76040 passes at 10.33 with 8E46, the 07.30 Warrington Arpley Yard to Tinsley mixed freight. *Paul Shannon*

Right: After the withdrawal of passenger services between Sheffield and Manchester in 1970, the once busy station at Penistone practically became a ghost town, with just an hourly DMU service linking Huddersfield and Sheffield. This Class 101 and Class 110 combination, which consists of vehicles 51432, 59811 & 51839, arrives from the Huddersfield direction; the service has only one passenger to collect at Penistone – the photographer!

Below: Barnsley Junction was just east of Huddersfield Junction and where the line for Wath and Barnsley left the line south to Sheffield. The route forward to Wath was electrified and included the steeply-graded Worsborough Incline. Taken on 4 March 1981, from the signal box at Barnsley Junction, this photograph shows 76007 and 76026 bringing their lengthy train off the Worsborough Incline and towards Penistone station. The working is 6M49, a loaded MGR train from Wath Yard to Fiddlers Ferry Power Station.

Above: These two images show 76034 & 76032 passing Barnsley Junction signal box with 6E38, an empty MGR working from Fiddlers Ferry Power Station to Wath Yard. As I recall, a pleasant interlude was spent in the signal box, which is interesting because the date of this photograph was 4 March 1981, yet the Signalling Record Society lists the box as closing on 2 January 1981. I suspect this is an error because the image of the train passing the box clearly shows the signalman climbing the box's steps. The building was opened in 1887, initially with 50 levers, before being expanded in 1957 to accommodate 90 levers. I suspect it actually closed in July 1981 with the electrified line. Sadly I never recorded an interior view of the box, in which myself and Paul Shannon spent at least an hour as guests of the signalman.

Above: 76013 & 76012 stand in the sidings at Penistone's Barnsley Junction on the morning of 4 March 1981. They are stuck there because it transpired that the guard of 6E32, which is the empty MGR working from Fiddlers Ferry to Wath that they were due to take forward, "didn't know the road" to Wath! "Why does an air-braked train need a guard?" you may ask. At the time BR's attempts to modernise the railway met strong resistance from staff and unions that didn't want to see positions such as guards on freight trains being withdrawn. Such restrictive practices and stubbornness back in the 1970s and '80s severely damaged the railway's share of freight haulage, as road transport offered much more flexibility.

Above: On 4 August 1978, 76023 passes Huddersfield Junction signal box with 6M36, an empty oil train from Ecclesfield in Sheffield to Stanlow Refinery in Cheshire. This service was diverted to run over the Hope Valley Line a couple of years later. *Paul Shannon*

Above: With a sprinkling of snow on the platform, 76008 and 76021 pass through Penistone station with an MGR working that is returning empty wagons from Fiddlers Ferry Power Station to Wath Yard on 7 January 1981. *Paul Shannon*

Above: Looking at the beer barrels on this freightliner service suggests that it is 4M55, the Newcastle to Trafford Park freightliner that included a healthy load of Newcastle Brown Ale for Manchester. It is seen passing Huddersfield Junction on 22 September 1980 behind 76015 and 76024. In the last year of the Woodhead Line, these freightliner services were usually hauled by a pair of Class 37s or a single Class 47, negating the need to change from diesel to electric traction, then back to diesel again during the middle of the journey. *Paul Shannon*

Above: On 29 October 1980, 76051 passes through Penistone station with 8E11, a mixed freight from Dewsnap Sidings to Tinsley. The front half of the train is made up of mineral wagons that are carrying scrap metal bound for the electric arc furnaces at Aldwarke Steelworks in Rotherham.

Above: 37209 arrives at Barnsley Junction from the west on 4 March 1981. Its next movement will be to back into the sidings in the background with "T70", the trip working from Dodworth Colliery. Taken from the signal box, this view shows that it is hauling a half-length MGR train of just 15 HAA hoppers, the shorter load being necessary due to the steep gradients within the Barnsley area. The two portions of the train will be shunted together here, before it crosses the Pennines behind a pair of Class 76s, which will then be exchanged for another diesel for the last leg to Fiddlers Ferry Power Station.

CHAPTER 5

Penistone to Tinsley and Rotherwood

Above: This sad view shows 31287 heading a track recovery train at Deepcar on 26 September 1985. The former main line has been reduced to a single track branch and the electrification equipment has been removed.

Above: Also at Deepcar on 26 September 1985, 08244 is seen stabled at the headshunt for the nearby Stocksbridge Steelworks, where it is out-stabled from Tinsley to act as the works pilot. The closed Deepcar station is visible in the background.

Above: In happier times for the Woodhead Line, 08813 heads into the steelworks at Stocksbridge with a couple of brake vans and some 16-ton mineral wagons that are carrying coal. Behind the locomotive is the main line, still electrified and double-tracked on 9 January 1981. *Paul Shannon*

Below: On 9 January 1981, 76040 heads towards Penistone as it passes the coal depot at Deepcar with a Rotherwood to Ashburys unfitted freight. *Paul Shannon*

Above: While making a light engine movement from Tinsley to Penistone on 12 January 1978, 76026 and 76027 are seen near the closed Sheffield Victoria station. My notebook records this was the day that I had a medical school interview at Sheffield University, so after the interview a few pictures were taken in Sheffield and at Tinsley depot before the light faded.

Above: Sheffield No. 4 signal box opened in 1902 and was enlarged to accommodate 110 levers in 1953 when the Woodhead Route was electrified. Modernisation in 1965 saw the number of levers reduced to 50 and a Westinghouse IFS panel installed. The box survived until 1986 and was the last remnant of Victoria station to be demolished.

Below: This sad view shows Sheffield Victoria during January 1978, eight years after its passenger services had been withdrawn, with a two-car Class 114 passing through the closed station.

Above: 76054 is captured at Nunnery Sidings, as seen from a passing Sheffield to Huddersfield train which had paused to reverse here. The locomotive is travelling light engine to the stabling point at Rotherwood.

Above: Further up the line towards Penistone, just north of Sheffield Victoria, 20004 and 20056 head south with a short train of air-braked wagons that they are moving from the Stocksbridge Steelworks to Tinsley Yard.

Class	Locomotives
08	08024, 08183, 08223, 08260, 08331, 08386, 08507, 08810 & 08879
13	13001, 13002 & 13003
20	20017, 20022, 20061, 20129, 20144 & 20145
31	31275 & 31300
37	37052, 37108, 37112, 37121, 37122 & 37126
45	45021, 45027, 45030, 45035, 45038 & 45061
47	47098, 47113, 47174, 47175 & 47307
56	56001, 56003, 56013 & 56018

Table 3: The locomotives that were present at Tinsley depot at 11.45 on 12 January 1978.

Above right: The eastern two extremities of the DC electrified network in the Sheffield area were Rotherwood and Tinsley. This view of the reception yard at Tinsley was taken on 12 January 1978 and shows the catenary which covered six of the reception sidings and one run-round road. 13003 and 13001 were both on hump shunting duty that day.

Right: 13003 has just finished humping its train and stands on the hump crest at Tinsley on 12 January 1978. The electrified arrival line on the left runs round the southern edge of the sorting sidings, to the south of the hump, and into the six reception tracks that are equipped with overhead electrification.

Opposite: These two views show 76051 leaving Tinsley with 8T30, a trip freight that is heading to Deepcar. The western end of the sorting sidings at Tinsley was partially electrified to allow departures for Woodhead to leave directly from the yard. In the receding view, the five express freight sidings can be seen beyond the locomotive and these were fully electrified, handling several trans-Pennine freights every evening during the 1960s and early 1970s.

Above: By 20 May 1985, all traces of the overhead electrification had gone from the express freight sidings at Tinsley which were used as a reception yard for the complex. Tinsley Park signal box controlled all movements in the area and the top left insert shows the signalman trying to concentrate as the shunters on duty chat between the arrivals. From left to right, the main image shows 08878, which has arrived with 8T32, a trip working from Broughton Lane Sidings, 20176 & 20098 on the 6T30 trip working from Deepcar and 20064 & 20015 with the 6T35 trip working from Aldwarke.

Above: 76022 and 76013 pass along the southern edge of the sorting sidings at Tinsley Yard as they arrive with 8E11, a mixed freight from Dewsnap Sidings on 23 September 1980.

Above: Just 23 minutes later and 76022 and 76013 are now seen at the rarely photographed Shepcote Lane Junction. Passing the western end of the express freight sidings, they are returning to Manchester light engine as there was no traffic ready for their return working to Dewsnap Sidings.

Above: 20209 and 20208 run onto the refuelling point at Tinsley. The catenary above the arrival track for Woodhead traffic can be seen, along with the wiring that would allow Class 76s to stable in the refuelling point (although they rarely did). Beyond the locomotives, at the far end of the large yard, the extensive overhead infrastructure at its western end can be seen stretching over the southern half of the sorting sidings and the secondary sorting sidings. A Class 31 that is about to depart westwards can just be discerned under the gantry that is securing the end of the overhead wires to the left in the background.

Left: The end of the wires at the eastern end of the Tinsley Yard complex is seen here on 23 September 1980. 45039 "The Manchester Regiment" is about to pass under the A630 dual carriageway with 8J12, a mixed freight that is running from Tees Yard to Tinsley.

Below left: On 9 September 1986, the former reception sidings at Tinsley make a sorry sight. The remains of the six electrified tracks are on the left in this view, which was taken from the A630 overbridge. In the centre, 47355 is seen heading for the main yard with 6V06, the Healey Mills to Severn Tunnel Junction Speedlink, which will collect traffic at Tinsley's main yard before heading south.

Below: This general view shows the yard and stabling point at Rotherwood during September 1980. Class 114 vehicles E56033 & E50036 pass a total of seven Class 76s that are stabled there, as they head west with a Cleethorpes to Sheffield service.

Left & below left: These two photographs show 20026 and 20031 passing the sidings at Rotherwood on 23 September 1980, with the bridge from which the previous view of the area was captured being visible in the background. The train is 8G78, a coal working from Worksop to Tinsley that will be sorted at Tinsley. There the wagons will be put on various mixed freights that will leave the yard that night to make their way to a variety of household coal depots all over the country. In the going away shot, to the left of the Class 20s, 76014 and 76027 can be seen stabled while they await their next duty.

Above: This close-up shows 76014 and 76027 stabled at Rotherwood sidings. Behind them 31278 and 31271 have just arrived, ready to haul the evening coke train from Orgreave Coke Works to Scunthorpe Steelworks.

Below: Oil originally from the refinery at Stanlow arrives at Rotherwood Sidings behind 37123 on 23 September 1980. The train is running as 6M38 from Wath and is destined for the East Midlands.

Above right: Much of the infrastructure at Rotherwood is displayed in this view of 31311 on 6T68, a trip working from Tinsley Yard to Beighton Permanent Way Depot, again on 23 September 1980. Orgreave Colliery signal box can be seen in the background; the box opened in 1901 with 75 levers which controlled access to the colliery and coke works of the same name, before being closed in 1985.

Below: On 30 September 1980, the driver of this Class 114 DMU, which comprises vehicles E50022 and E56044, looks quizzically at the two photographers who are perched on the embankment opposite Orgreave Colliery Sidings, as he passes with a Sheffield to Cleethorpes passenger service.

CHAPTER 6

Penistone to Wath Central

The chapter documents the north-eastern arm of the Woodhead Route that ran from Penistone to Wombwell Main Junction and the depot and marshalling yard at Wath.

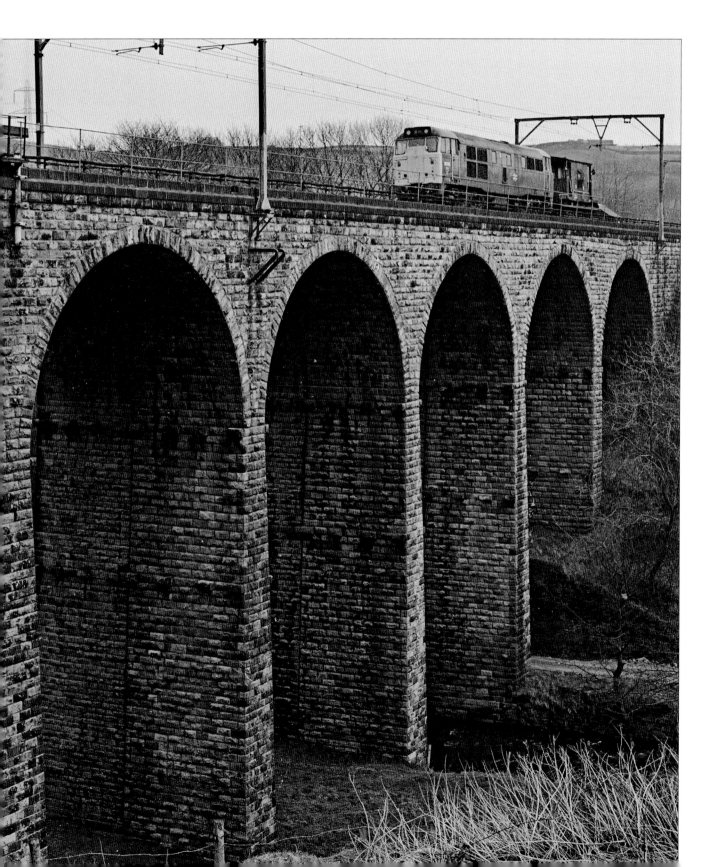

Left, right & below: 4 March 1981 was an epic day out for myself and fellow photographer Paul Shannon, beginning with us leaving Cambridge at 01.14 and we returned there at 22.58. The day was spent cycling along the course of the Penistone to Wath section of the Woodhead Route and the first images of the day were taken at Oxspring Viaduct and the nearby Oxspring Tunnel. Firstly 31116 is seen crossing Oxspring Viaduct as it runs "engine and van" as the "T90" shunt from Wath Yard to Penistone. Then from the parapet over Oxspring Tunnel, an unidentified pair of Class 76s head west with a loaded Wath to Fiddlers Ferry MGR service. Finally 76026 and 76007 are seen making their way in the other direction with an empty MGR working from Fiddlers Ferry to Wath Yard.

Above: 76006 and 76024 are banking, while 76007 and 76026 lead 6M55, the loaded MGR working from Wath to Fiddlers Ferry Power Station, through Kendall Green. The signal box here is shown in the inset, with Paul Shannon rummaging in his bag for another roll of film. The box dates back to 1924 when it replaced an older 1889 structure. It had just nine mechanical levers and closed with the line on 20 July 1981.

Above: The signal box at Worsboro' Bridge Crossing also opened in 1924 to replace an older box. It had 14 levers and is seen in the distance in this view of 76024 and 76006, as they return light engine from Silkstone to Wath Yard after having banked the MGR train seen in the previous photograph.

Above: 76024 and 76006 are now seen a few hundred yards further on, as they pass Glasshouse Crossing. It is interesting to see how high their pantographs have extended, this being because the wires here had been elevated to provide as much height as possible for road traffic to cross the railway. The crossing keeper's box also opened in 1924, originally with 15 levers, but by 1981 the number had reduced to just nine. Like all the boxes along the Worsborough Incline, it closed on 20 July 1981 when the line was shut for good.

Above: 76034 and 76032 pass Lewden Crossing with 6E31, an empty MGR working from Fiddlers Ferry to Wath. The signal box here opened in 1904, when it replaced an 1880 structure, and it had 15 levers.

Opposite top & bottom: Across the valley floor from Lewden Crossing was the Rockingham branch and just as we were leaving Lewden a pair of Class 20s whistled into view. A hurried cycle up the hill found 20029 and 20031 with the afternoon trip working from Barrow Colliery to Wath Yard. The first photograph shows them ambling past the edge of Dovecliffe signal box, a relatively modern structure that opened in 1974 with 21 levers. The box had a short life, as it would be closed just eight years later in 1982. The other image shows 20132 and 20004 passing nearby Wombwell Main Junction during April 1980, running light engine from Wath Yard to the colliery; it was this working that alerted us to these trip freights to and from Barrow Colliery 11 months before we photographed 20029 and 20031.

Above: Returning to 4 March 1981, the afternoon trip working to Wath Yard leaves Barrow Colliery and heads away from the photographer behind 20031 and 20029, as seen from the footbridge over Dovecliffe Level Crossing.

The next five images form a sequence that shows 76022 and 76023 as they arrive at the banking station at Wombwell Main Junction on 4 March 1981. After a signal check by the signal box they eased into the banking station, where 76024 and 76006 were waiting, ahead of being attach to the rear of the train. As was so often the way, Paul's film had run out at the wrong moment, so he can be seen scrambling to change film while the train creeps past Wombwell Main Junction signal box. Next, as the loaded MGR train passes the banking locomotives, the driver of the bankers walks to his engines after having stopped to chat to us and invite us to ride with him up to West Silkstone and back. Speedy negotiations were then made with the signalman who kindly agreed to look after our bicycles. After having thought our day out was over, we then embarked on our unexpected cab ride up the Worsborough Incline to West Silkstone Junction and back!

Right: As we rattled up the incline pushing 6M57, a Wath to Fiddlers Ferry MGR, the light faded, making photography a challenge. Our driver can be seen leaning out of his window as we ascended the incline, while we took pictures from 76006's other cab window.

Above: The 1880 vintage signal box at West Silkstone Junction is seen from the cab of our banking locomotives as we return to Wombwell. The windscreen wasn't particularly clean, which explains why the image isn't very sharp. The upper insert shows the 33-lever signal box as we arrive and just before our MGR train eases away towards Penistone. The signal box here closed on 17 August 1981, slightly after the Woodhead Route was shut, a reflection of the nearby branch line to Dodworth Colliery. The lower insert shows fellow photographer Paul Shannon as we change ends for the light engine movement back to Wombwell Main Junction where our bicycles awaited.

Below left: This is one of my favourite images of the Woodhead Route and was captured at Kendall Green Crossing on 4 March 1981. 76007 & 76026 head 6M55, a Wath to Fiddlers Ferry MGR that is being banked between Wombwell Main Junction and West Silkstone Junction by 76006 & 76024. This is another shot from our 22-hour day trip from Cambridge, when we took our bikes with us so we could cycle between locations like this to photograph the latter-day movements on this part of the electrified line.

These next three photos were taken on 15 April 1980, when we made another long day trip from Cambridge. My notebook tells me that this started with the 05.50 from Cambridge to Peterborough, where we arrived at 07.00 to catch the 05.50 Kings Cross–Aberdeen which was hauled by 55016. This arrived in Doncaster at 08.15, then the 08.37 was taken to Mexborough where we alighted with our bicycles. We then cycled to Wombwell, stopping at Wath Road on the Midland Main Line, Manvers Coking Plant, Wath Yard, Elsecar Junction and finally Wombwell Main Junction. Later that day there was a frantic cycle back to Mexborough for the 17.12 to Doncaster. We left Doncaster at 17.34 behind 55007 on the 16.30 Hull–King's Cross, changing at Peterborough to arrive back in Cambridge at 20.43.

Above: 76014 & 76008 were the bankers for MGR services on 15 April 1980 and are seen arriving back at Wombwell Main Junction after working on the Worsborough Incline. They will park up on the tracks seen in the lower left area, where they will await their next train.

Above: 76036 & 76039 pass Wombwell Main Junction signal box with the afternoon Wath to Dewsnap Sidings mixed freight. The signal box here opened in 1905 and contained a 53-lever frame. An IFS Panel was added in 1951 as part of the Woodhead electrification and the box finally closed on 14 February 1982 when coal traffic from the nearby Barrow Colliery ceased.

Above: Usually there would just be one pair of Class 76s outposted at Wombwell Main Junction for banking duties, but on this particular date, 15 April 1980, I was presented with the unusual sight of three bankers there.

Above: The signal box at Mitchells Main was just three miles up the line from Wath Yard towards Wombwell. It looked a sorry sight on 26 September 1985, after the surrounding electrification equipment had been removed and the box had been switched out; it wasn't officially closed until November 1985, but had already been vandalised.

Above: On 15 April 1980, a group of four or five of us that had travelled from Cambridge spent an enjoyable couple of hours in Elsecar Junction signal box. This was just west of Wath Yard and where the branch to Elsecar Main Colliery began, as seen on the left. 40002 passes with 8K22, a working from Healey Mills to Wath Yard.

Above: 37135 passes Elsecar Junction with T63, a trip working from Cortonwood Colliery, which was Arthur Scargill's former place of employment. The signalman is about to accept the single line token for the colliery branch. The signal box at Elsecar Junction opened in 1891, replacing an earlier 1880-built structure. It had 64 levers and as I recall (although I did not photograph them), they were Great Central miniature levers. An IFS Panel was added in 1951 to control access to the electrified depot and the box finally closed on 17 November 1985.

Right & above right: 76049 is seen from the signal box at Elsecar Junction as it approaches Wath Yard with 7E00, a partially-fitted mineral working from Ashburys Yard. Readers may think I have perhaps captured the train too far away and they would be correct; my contemporaneous notes remind me that there was such a crush among the photographers clamouring to take a picture through the window that my second frame with the train closer had half a window frame obscuring the view! I did however have time to raise my second camera and get a colour slide a moment later.

Above: 76049 has had a relatively quick turnaround as it sets out from Wath Yard on 15 April 1980 with 8M17, a loaded coal train that is destined for Ashburys. It had only passed Elsecar Junction at 12.11 and is now returning west with a coal train at 12.50. The coal had arrived in Wath Yard earlier that morning as the 8T61 trip from Grimethorpe Colliery.

Above: This general view of the western entrance to Wath Yard at Elsecar Junction shows 76029 & 76030 and their train weaving their way onto the through lines that bypassed the marshalling yard with 8E08, a working from Wallerscote to Rockware. This conveyed soda ash to the Rockware glassworks in Doncaster.

Above: Whilst it is slightly outside of the timeframe of this book, I have included this photograph of Wath depot as it was taken during my first visit there on 22 July 1974. Here we see 76056, along with four of its classmates. 76056 was one of the earlier withdrawals, being taken out of service in 1978.

Above: On 15 April 1980, 76035, 76038, 76006, 76021, 76022 and 76013 were all lined up on Wath electric depot, with the pantographs of the nearest two locomotives having been lowered.

Left: Again on 15 April 1980, 76022 & 76013 trundle away from the depot at Wath to go and pick up a heavy rake of MGRs that are loaded with coal. Their load will be taken westwards and ultimately burned to produce electricity at Fiddlers Ferry Power Station.

Right: 20059 & 20005 are seen from the road overbridge at the eastern end of Wath Yard as they set out from the sorting sidings with a lengthy rake of 16-ton mineral wagons that are loaded with scrap metal. The train is bound initially for Tinsley. Some of the Class 76s that are stabled on the depot can be seen on the right.

Below: 45026 makes its way out of Wath Yard and past Wath Central signal box on 16 March 1982 with the 6T22 trip to Hickelton Colliery. The signal box here opened in 1907, replacing an older cabin that dated back to 1880 and was built as part of the much larger project to construct Wath Yard. It contained 65 levers and went on to close on 24 July 1988. Wath Central marked the eastern end of the Woodhead Route in the Wath area.

Above & below: When I visited Wath on 16 March 1982, even though the Woodhead Line had closed the previous summer and electric services had ceased, the yard was still relatively busy. The disused overhead catenary was still in-situ nine months after it was last used, as seen on the right. 08434 was shunting in the sorting sidings, making up what will become 8T61, the trip freight to Healey Mills Yard. In the distance 31220 has just arrived to take this forward to Healey Mills; it will reverse out of the yard towards Manvers before heading north-west to Healey Mills. The second image looks in the other direction and shows 31220 after it propelled the train out of the yard and passed Moor Road Bridge signal box, the roof of which can be seen in the bottom right. This box controlled access to the yard with its 32 levers and closed just over three months later, on 4 July 1982. The skyline is dominated by the winding gear of Manvers Main Colliery and the furnaces of Manvers Coking Plant.

Left & below: By September 1985, much of Wath Yard had been done away with and it was on its last legs. A solitary 08782 was on hand to shuttle back and forth to the nearby Manvers Coking Plant as the 6T30 trip working. 20167 & 20174 were awaiting departure with 6T36, a Speedlink coal working for Tinsley that was made up of HEA hoppers. The wider-angle panorama shows the extent of the dereliction. Most of the once-busy yard had become wasteland and the sorry-looking former electric depot on the right had been repurposed as an industrial unit. The yard closed completely a year later and today there is no hint of the former railway in Wath, as the entire site is now covered by a combination of housing and an industrial estate.

Above: About half a mile to the east of Wath Central signal box, the overbridge at the eastern end of Wath Yard can just be seen through the morning mist. On 15 April 1980, 20004 & 20132 head a rake of empty 16-ton mineral wagons past "Wath Jc" signal box. The nameboard is a shortening of the signal box's full name, which is Wath Central Junction. It opened in 1882 and contained 50 levers and closed on 10 May 1981.

Above: This final image of the railway to the east of Wath Yard shows 20059 & 20005 as they head east with a rake of empty steel carriers. The signal box on the right is Staithe Crossing which opened in 1907 and lies less than a mile from Wath Marshalling Yard. Its 28 levers fell silent on 10 May 1981.